Healing With Light Language - Energy Healing and Ascension with Wisdom for Body, Soul, and Spirit

Table Of Contents

Introduction

Have you ever really listened to the way you talk to people? Have you truly listened to the way you speak?

What is it like?

Whenever I hear my voice, I feel strange. Is that really me? Recorded voices are even weirder, like disembodied little pieces of me. My voice sounds like it is coming from afar.

But language has never really been limited by voice. It is a medium of communication that connects you to someone else. Speech can be constrained by culture, but it can also be free to transform into something else. We have sign language, Braille, and other forms that transcend different types of ability.

However, nothing is like the light language. Light language is a means of communication that is more spiritual than intellectual. It connects you to a Higher Being or the Universe instead of merely connecting you to another human.

This book will help you:

- Define and understand light language
- Use light language to heal various types of conditions
- Ascend in wisdom and the spirit
- Pass on your knowledge to others who need it

Chapter 1 – History of the Language of Light

Everything has a beginning. There was a time nobody really cared enough to talk about transcendence. But there is also a time that came before that when everything is one little ball of light.

> *"The language of light can only be decoded by the heart".*
>
> *Suzy Kassem*

We can be sure that for a time, people just want to satisfy their basic necessities.

During the time of the cavemen, a lot of emphasis was made on the physicality of leaders. Leaders must be strong so that they can lead their people in battle. They can also more easily take down a wild boar, for example.

A language was not as important as physical communication at that time. So, yes, we are not exactly sure if cavemen communicated in grunts. Still, we know that they were more focused on surviving.

They wrote their stories, too. That cannot be

The biblical story of the Tower of Babel tried to explain away the disparity in human languages

denied. Cave paintings gave us a peek of

The biblical story of the Tower of Babel tried to explain away the disparity in human languages. It said that humans were too proud that they should not be allowed to communicate and work together. The successful building of the tower would have meant reaching the heavens.

At that time, reaching the heavens was considered blasphemy. The attitudes of the people who were aiming for the skies were that of pride. They were attempting to be higher than God.

But that is not what the language of light is. This language is not operating in the absence of God. Instead, it is thought to be the language of angels. It vibrates in the positive energy of being in a heavenly presence. It does not have problems with connecting with the higher power.

Throughout history, in numerous cultures,

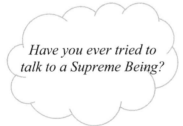

Have you ever tried to talk to a Supreme Being?

there are variations of the light language. People have always been interested in connecting to a Higher Being. They feel that this is how to achieve their own higher self – and a sense of peace.

You will find someone calling out to a deity through dance. Others would sit in stillness, making contact with the elements. These little appeals are representations of the language of light. They can be found in both religious and non-religious practices.

Chapter 2 – What is the Language of Light?

The language of light is used to communicate beyond human means.

If you can speak, you know that spoken words are not always successful. Yes, it gets you by and gets you around. However, it can also put you in trouble. People can misunderstand what you are trying to say.

> *Based on our natural heritage as the Divine Light of God every one of us possesses intuition... defined as the language of the soul.*
>
> *- James Van Praagh*

Humans have also added another limitation, and that is language. People all around the world speak various languages. Even within a country, people may have several dialects. Moreover, the dialects can further evolve into multiple subtypes.

Normally, language is supposed to be an aid. However, it has become more like a barrier when two people who speak different languages meet.

Instead of helping people connect, these variants continue to separate. We've heard about polyglots who have mastered several languages. They could

> *Papua New Guinea is the country with the most number of languages in the world. It has 841 languages.*
>
> *- Speakt*

speak to more people, as a result. Unfortunately, not everyone has that capability. As a human grows older, the capacity to learn new languages decreases, as well.

Many people also depend on a medium language. This is a language that works as a channel between two completely different ones. English is often this particular language of choice. Even then, things can still get lost in translation. Translation attempts to bridge the gap but fails to express the lived-in feeling of each culture. It sometimes does not show what goes on beyond the words and their literal meanings. This is why good translators should know what it is like to live in the culture of the two languages they are trying to tie together.

The language of light transcends this limitation. It can use multiple channels. You can speak it, write it, and even feel it with vibration.

With vibration, you can reach more. That thrumming energy within you makes you capable of communicating with people and with a higher power – or, more practically, with your higher self.

This is the language of light. It is not a set of words with a specialized alphabet. This language is meant to communicate and heal, improve, and help you ascend. Ascension has a lot to do with you achieving your full potential.

What is the difference between learning languages and immersing in light language?

The difference between attempting to become a polyglot and ascending through the language of light is clear. It is challenging to even master three languages. Some people can barely even speak two, while others content themselves with one. However, ascension in the language of light is possible for anyone.

Anyone can tap into their higher self through the language of light. You just need to be exposed to a practitioner or healer. This is not something that you can learn just by reading a book. However, a book can at least guide you as to what to expect.

This is why this book is here for you.

You can achieve your highest potential through the language of light.

It does not matter what your background is like. It does not matter if you speak one language or more. Your intellectual capacity will not be called into account – because it is your spirit, not your logic, that will make the connection.

If you talk to someone about the light language, some of them will scoff at you. These people will demand scientific explanations for what you are doing. But, if you mull it over, they have a point. They just want to understand. So, they are hoping for some tangible proof.

But you need to let go of this mindset for you to immerse yourself in the light language. Just like the energy that it is named for, it can bathe you with energy. It will bring you towards completion and clarity.

So while human languages are more easily defined, logic is not as much needed in light language. The rules of human languages are clear, collected in textbooks, and taught via modules. On the other hand, light language is more felt than learned. You discover every aspect of it when you have already begun to practice it.

What is the difference between speaking in tongues and light language?

Speaking in tongues has so much in common with light language. Both mean talking in a language that you have not formally learned.

The difference may be in your faith. If you are working within the context of a religious community – especially a Christian sect. In this sect, people believe in a dogmatic god. Speaking in tongues is often associated with the Holy Spirit coming down and inspiring people.

Light language is not much different. You are calling upon an astral entity when you speak in this light language. However, the vibe that you get is more cultural and genetic. You are not looking high up in the heavens. Instead, you are looking inside yourself for whatever is already imprinted there.

Is light language a subgroup of any other language?

It is a non-earthly language. When you utter the words, you will not understand them. Even the ones listening to you will wonder what you are trying to say. However, as they keep on listening, they will start hearing it as a language. By then, it is no longer gibberish. Strangely, some practitioners said that the words that come out of their mouth have the same patterns as an existing language, which they have never learned in school. The words just come flowing. Other people notice the similarity in patterns, as well.

Why is it easier to talk in the language of light?

Well, it is because you can make use of your own channel to successfully communicate.

What are ways in which you can express light language?

Do you like to converse? Then, you can speak the language of light. You can take advantage of the natural gift of the speech given to you. Use your voice to communicate to the Universe.

But not everyone likes to talk.

Do you like to dance, instead? Some people would rather express their stories and emotions through dance. They use their limbs to sway and connect to the Universe. But, again, you are playing to your ability. You may have noticed that several cultures have used this ability to connect to a Higher Being. Others may even dismiss the practice as pagan and barbaric. You will discover that this is not the case. People just have varying ways of communication.

Do you like to use sign language? Well, you can make the most of it and connect using a language you feel confident in. You can communicate to a higher power even if you have to keep things silent. Using sign language when you are not deaf also conveys an openness to other people. You know that you must try to reach out to more people. This type of openness will make it easier for you to converse in the language of the angels.

Do you like to listen to binaural beats while you meditate? Then, this is a way for you to connect yourself to the heavens, as well. Find your mind and soul attracting the cosmos. Binaural beats can change not just the rhythm of your heart but also the vibration of your soul. You will delve into this further in this book.

You can express yourself through all of the above because the language of light is the language of the soul.

When you speak this language, you bypass human logic. You have decided to skip all that constraints you as a human. So, you connect through the soul.

Because it connects with the soul and is all about communicating a particular vibration, this language can also create change and healing.

What does this language feel like?

Just like with any language, the effect on people will vary. What you feel right now will be different from what other people may feel.

However, here are some common effects of the language of light:

- A feeling of freeness and libration
- Warmth or coolness, something that can be distinctly separated from the rest of what you are feeling
- Tingling and muscle twisting
- Relaxation/reduced anxiety or stress
- A sudden burst or a gradual rise of energy
- Expanding of your senses
- Opening of your third Eye
- Getting in touch with your soul's purpose and essence
- A flash of memory, feeling, or inspiration

Again, you don't have to feel anything in particular. Do not feel bothered if you are simply feeling like your regular self. Healing and ascension can happen without you feeling anything physical. Eventually, you will feel a lifting of all your burdens. You will feel like you can do anything. That is what being touched by the light language is all about.

Why should you try to communicate through light language?

As with any type of light, this language is born to take us away from the darkness.

While it is a heavenly language, its origins are darker. People who have found themselves buried in different problems are the ones who will likely seek the comfort of this means of communication.

When people are in utter despair, it is difficult for them to imagine a way of rising. They have lost hope and are trying to find something – a beacon that will help them out of the mire.

Sadly, in life, most of the time, we only seek the light when we have known darkness.

It is true we cannot generalize. Some of you may have grabbed this book because you want a healthy life, continuous progress from beginning to end. You may even be hoping to ascend to your highest self. For others, you are seeking comfort and healing. The illness may be physical, mental, or even spiritual. But whatever it may be, it is keeping you from achieving your full potential.

This language is here to carry you away from the dark despair you may be in. If this is not the case, it seeks to empower you and help you reach your dreams. Whatever the case may be, it aims to armor you with its ability to connect you to the Universe. Sometimes, we cannot do it alone. We need the guidance of a higher power. But we should also not forget that we are not completely helpless. The Universe is only taking what is already there and making it more powerful.

But you must recognize it – and you must communicate it. This has to be done through light language. Not everyone may understand it, but if you seek it – you will find it. Light language is multidimensional and is capable of making itself known to every type of person.

Why are there many facets to light language?

You are probably wondering why you can communicate in so many different ways. Yet, it will still be considered light language.

Less than one in 10 Indigenous Yukoners can speak or understand an Indigenous language, and young people across the North were far less likely to understand even a few words than their parents' generation.

Well, light language is about being certain of your destiny. It is about knowing that you are here for a purpose. Some people cannot even connect with human languages. Imagine going beyond that.

Acknowledging that purpose makes it easy for you to connect point A and point B.

With light language, the connection goes through the cosmos. It connects you to what should be your main purpose here on Earth – to expand your consciousness.

When you expand your consciousness, you will realize that being here is not even enough. You must continue finding comfort and healing beyond earthly goods can give.

Being one with the cosmos and taking what you need from it is what brings you balance.

What does this language have to do with light?

Languages are named accordingly. When you travel to a foreign land, you are more likely to hear of a different language aptly named after its country.

For example, you will hear the Russian language in Russia. The language's name will, of course, have its own name in its native land. In this case, it would be Ruskiy. While there may be variations in how we call these languages, we can still trace the etymology.

This is the same with light.

The light language is thus named due to a few things. One, it bathes you in light. Therefore, you forget about all the darkness that may have tried to take over your being. Two, it is a quick means of communication – like going at the speed of light.

In summary, light language is a quick way to enlighten yourself. Once you know how to use it, it connects you to the Source. This is a bigger source than the sun. This is where all energy comes from. So, you can be uplifted and made to feel whole again.

I know. I know. Most of us think of the Internet when we think of fast responding communication. With just a click, you can send a message to someone who lives thousands of miles away.

But the light language is not just about sending a message. You also get the response you need immediately, especially if you have mastered tapping into the Universe.

Yeah, you will probably still say, "Oh, but I get that kind of communication with a close friend of mine." The back and forth can also be rapid. However, it is still an earthly and logical communication. Think about how different it would be if you connect – not to another human but to a Supreme Being or even the Universe. Before you can even put your requests in words, it is already known. The more free and connected you are, willing and able to open up, the faster the communication will be.

How did I become involved in the light language?

Everyone who talks about light language has somehow been touched by it.

In my case, there was a period of loss that made me seek the light. Imagine days when you feel like there is no reason to live.

Have you felt something like this? There will be days when you simply exist, not knowing why you have to get up the following day.

The opposite can be true.

Every day is painful. You are either constantly battling a physical illness or a mental burden.

Whatever the case may be, your consciousness is clouded and confused. You cannot communicate well physically because of your burdens.

It was like that for me.

Talking to someone had become a chore. I just wanted to be in my one little corner, away from everyone else. It was depression, my doctor said. The pills helped a little, but I was back to my black hole whenever the effects were gone.

Being in that state separated me from so many people. So, I had no hopes of even being connected to them spiritually and beyond.

Then, I heard about light language. A close friend would help me connect even if I am no longer comfortable with regular speaking. She was very earnest about her recommendation, which has been fueled by her belief in Shiva.

How would you best express yourself?

At first, I was hesitant. I was not particularly religious. So, I thought it would not work for me. Still, my friend was not insistent, but she said it would work out no matter my background. It was probably her calmness that sold it out for me.

Today, I could not say that I have fully ascended. While you are still alive, you are still going through the journey.

I am still in the process of healing. However, there has been a vast improvement in seeing the world after I learned how to look at it beyond its worldly form. I finally discovered how I could make myself go beyond the trap my mind had set upon me.

The next chapter should see you through your own journey towards healing using the language of light.

How will light language benefit you?

Why do people even delve into light language? Light language offers so many benefits to your body and soul:

- Supports you in your journey towards ascension or self-actualization
- Lifts you into a higher state of consciousness
- Reawakens your soul's memory
- Boosts your intuition
- Restores your physical, mental, and spiritual well-being
- Connects you to your forgotten Divinity by making you converse in a heavenly language

- Balances your chakra system
- Get rids of blockages and energy issues
- Unites us with our multidimensional self

Chapter 3 – Healing through Light Language

Light language is the medium of the divine. It is used to connect you to a Supreme Being. But what exactly can this type of connection do to benefit you?

Light language is the medium of the divine. It is used to connect you to a Supreme Being.

Being connected to a higher power enables you to tap into its healing powers. Some may say that it is only about digging deep into what the mind can do. However, it does more than that.

Light language is all about being able to heal the body through healing the mind first.

While light language is not attached to logic, as first mentioned, it does have a real effect on the body.

How does light language heal?

Light language heals the body by appealing to harmony.

When the body is in harmony, it more easily leans towards good health.

Light language is all about keeping things in harmony. A healthy lifestyle is similar to it in this way because it keeps everything within you in order – at a balance.

This language also unclogs some of the same spaces within your spirit that get stuck. When your chakras get blocked, you find yourself stuck in one place in real life, as well. Light language is capable of removing these blockages.

Have you ever encountered light language?

Before you can open yourself to the possibility of being healed by light language, think about a time when you may have encountered it.

Have you ever heard something or felt
something that you cannot completely explain
but made such a deep impact on you that you
feel a rush of emotions? For example, imagine
hearing someone mumble a series of words,
and then you start crying because of it.

You may have just encountered language.

If you are a Christian, you may have read the
story about Pentecost. The Holy Spirit comes
down upon the Apostles, and they start
speaking in languages. Some people interpret
this as a deconstruction of the Tower of Babel

> *If you talk to a man in a
> language he understands,
> that goes to his head. If you
> talk to him in his language,
> that goes to his heart.*
>
> - *Nelson Mandela*

story. However, instead of people getting
separated by varying languages, unity ensues
because the Apostles found themselves
speaking in tongues. At that point, they gained
the ability to understand languages that they

had never even studied. So, they could explore the world and preach the Good News.

This phenomenon is not solely found in Christianity. You will find some tribal or ritualistic practices. For example, a "medium" of sorts would start chanting and get into a trance and start speaking in a language nobody else in the group could understand. Usually, those who are there would find themselves overwhelmed by emotions that they could not understand. This must be why some people believe themselves healed after a healer had just chanted on them. The healer could have done it for the sick person, or the latter could have done it for himself in his desire to get better. That trembling feeling of faith is what could have moved him to heal himself with the use of his connection to a Supreme Being.

Here, you will see that something so inherently illogical can have some effect on your health and well-being. But, unfortunately, many people may put the practice down just because they cannot understand what is going on.

Can you create your own energy through light language?

Yes, you can. Each person has a certain level of vibration. At first, I had to get my friend to help me trigger my vibration. Then, she used her light language to help connect me to the Universe. Finally, she used to sing over me. It was funny at; first, I had to admit. I even thought that "Oh, this is how I am going to get healed out of my depression. A little humor comes a long way."

It was a serious matter, though. I felt humbled when I realized that I was making fun of something that I could not fully understand at that time.

During the next few sessions, though, I started connecting to the various rhythms. It was then that I forgot about the fact that I had no idea what my mentor was chanting. Instead, there was just this comforting feeling that started washing over me. What I appreciated about myself was that it did not matter where I was from. It also did not matter where she was from. We did not have to understand the words that were coming out of her mouth.

The important thing was that she was connecting to something deep within me.

As you keep getting exposed to someone who knows the light language, you become more in tune with what it must feel like. People have varying reactions to light language. Do not worry if you are progressing a little more slowly compared to others. However, you should make sure you are ready to bare your soul and open yourself up to emotions.

Is there only one way to heal the soul through light language?

Light languages can vary. Some will sound like actual dialects but do not really mean anything. Others do have meaning, according to healers who tend to mix them all up in a session. There is no explicit intention from the beginning. The healer just lets go of logic and inhibition and focuses on what the spiritual world expresses through her. I am only using the pronoun "her" because most of the healers I have encountered are female. However, it must be clear that the practice is not exclusive to women. Light languages are inclusive. They do not discriminate in gender, nationality, social status, and more.

Other healers use sounds and vibrations. Therefore, you will hear some light language recordings as a series of pulses and tics instead of voices and chanting. Any of these sounds can help you achieve a higher vibration.

The tics, pulses, and voices can all blend to create one continuous chant that connects you to the Universe. Even the connection to a higher being is not limited by a deity. Some would simply call out to a higher being, while others may call out to Jeshua or Shiva.

As I have mentioned earlier, my not being religious has not affected my ability to start this light language journey. However, as I progressed, I began believing that a higher being exists to create order in the Universe. I felt it. Most times, I could not put these into words. However, the feeling had become so strong that I could barely remember a time when I never believed. I just knew that there was that time.

The depression did not lift up after the first session. The gradual but undoubtedly progressive change happened, though.

So, are light languages only expressed in sound?

Sound is the most effective way to go about it because it directly affects the person's vibrations being healed. However, some healers also make use of healing symbols.

Healing symbols take the form of drawn visuals, as guided by a deity. For example, Lord Shiva has passed on the message about a Trinity Healing symbol. The Supreme Being has given the meaning behind this symbol.

The triad is common in religion. For example, Christianity (especially Catholicism) recognizes the trinity of Father, Son, and Holy Spirit. Lord Shiva's trinity comprises what most supreme beings are about: creator, nurturer, and destroyer.

The Supreme Being is a creator. Everything around you will not have been made if not for your deity. So, He knows what it is like to connect these entities together. When you call out towards the heavens, using light language, you seek help in uniting these entities.

The Supreme Being is a nurturer. He is the one you must seek if you want to continue to thrive and grow. He is the one who can provide you

Would it matter to you if a session focuses on a particular deity?

with healing. Your light language healer can connect you to Him. In fact, you can make the connection on your own after you have mastered the light language.

The Supreme Being is a destroyer. Some stories about Supreme Beings talk about how they destroy to cleanse. The Flood story is about that. It is about rebirth and not about hate and total destruction.

Don't worry. When you find yourself immersed in light language, the only things that will be destroyed are the ones that were pulling you down and making you miserable.

This was what happened to me. I felt the creation and destruction at the same time. I may not remember my own birth, but I was completely lucid during my rebirth. It was the time that I felt all the weight of my depression lifting up from me.

Holding the trinity symbol is often not enough, though. You still have to tap on the vibrations. One way to do this is by chanting, "Om Namah Shivaya." The rest of the chants do not have to hold meaning. As you become more experienced, you will know when it is right to add more chants.

Light language is expressed in other symbols, too.

Lord Shiva has revealed a symbol that is specifically known as a letter of dissolution. This symbol focuses on the destruction part. First, however, it must be made clear that you are only meant to destroy the factors that you do not really need. You can also add in the parts that may ruin you if they remain.

So, now you know that even if there is a lot of focus on manifestation, you can also un-manifest things. Whatever you create, you can also destroy. In so doing, you have taken on the cape of a supreme being in your own right. You are in control.

Therefore, with the help of the dissolution symbol, you can destroy the unhealthy practices that you have found yourself engaged in. For example, eating salty and sugary foods may have resulted in poor health. You may have hoped for more delicious foods at one point as part of your wealth manifestation. You don't have to keep every possible aspect and result of the wealthier life provided by the Universe.

You can let go.

Not everything you wished for turned out to be that good. It may be disappointing and even anticlimactic. However, it will also teach you about who you are and what you really want in life.

In the end, you will realize that if something is not good for you, you must let go as early as you can. This way, you can keep yourself healthy.

Are there several symbols associated with light language healing?

Yes, there are countless symbols out there that can be used to invoke healing. You will find something new with each reference to accompany the sounds you have chosen to emanate and trigger the right vibrations.

Flower of Life

For example, the flower of life is one healing symbol you may be interested in. It is made up of overlapping circles. The pattern is intricate, just like the Universe. This soul-flower pattern is the definition of creation and unity, as each petal joins with the others.

When you are healing, you are recreating and building. Your body is attempting to get back into harmony. So, your light language session may need a sigil like this.

Metatron's Cube

Another symbol that highlights the healing process is Metatron's Cube. The three-dimensional cube can be found inside a circle. This circle enables it to spin, gaining enough momentum to shed negative energy and embrace positivity.

If your problem is mental and emotional, you may want to use this cube as your sigil. It will help you get rid of unwanted thoughts that may have continued to plague you.

Do you always need to understand the symbols?

As with the actual words and chants used, the answer to this question is "no." Again, you don't have to understand the logic of the symbols. However, you will feel it. As with the words, you may not feel anything during the first session. Do not beat yourself up about it, and do not descend into despairing doubt, either.

What is a light language healing session like?

Because of its inclusive nature, light language may vary in structure and result. So, one healer may differ in ritual from another. If you decide to go through the healing session independently, you will also encounter some differences.

If you search for some recordings, you may be given snippets on healers' websites or even on YouTube. A typical session, however, may last for 60 minutes. Having the same duration with another client does not mean you will have the same progress. One may feel lifted up at the end, while another will still feel confused and wonder what can happen next.

Remember, every person's experience is unique. Some may just need a little nudge, guidance towards the light. These are people who are temporarily stressed and troubled. A single event may have triggered a sense of sadness, shock, or distress. Otherwise, their lives may be peaceful enough.

For some people, the trauma clings to them tightly. They struggle to even listen to external voices. It is challenging to get out of the box that they have enclosed themselves in.

Other people may also be looking for physical healing. Psychosomatic symptoms may respond more quickly than critical physical ones.

Psychosomatic refers to a physical condition brought about by a mental one. For example, if you are stressed out, you will feel all kinds of symptoms, such as insomnia, pains, diarrhea, and more. Light language sessions can easily target the mental and emotional. Their vibrations can make an emotional connection from the very first meeting. On the other hand, physical diagnosis cannot be simply cured by a few sessions.

It does not mean it is impossible.

Many physical diseases are the result of a clogged chakra. You can then direct the vibrations towards that chakra. Then, express your vocal light language directly on that focal point, even using sigils that could get rid of negativity.

During your one-hour session with your healer, she will ask you if you have a personal healing intention.

Now, some may not like this. These seekers believe that if the Universe is truly listening, then the healer is all-knowing.

But that is not how it works.

When you express your personal healing intention, you give voice to your true need. When you acknowledge the assistance that you require, it shows your awareness of the matter. It also puts the request out there. The request can be chanted or written on a piece of paper.

Two main things happen when you acknowledge your personal healing intention. One, you put your request out there. By being fully conscious of this choice, you have made a decision to heal yourself. Two, you are giving your healer more information. She will then know what type of light language will work the best for you. This is just like going to a medical doctor and talking about your complaint. You cannot expect something that you have not explicitly asked for.

Your hour with your healer will be spent with her transmitting to you the sounds of light language. Next, she will take a sigil and place it on the part of your body that needs to be treated. Then, she will chant. Light language is not limited to the song format. So, your healer may also sometimes talk. Her gentle voice will make the words sound like chants, though, and the overall effect is that of prayer or ritual.

What is light language activation?

When your healer goes over your intention and starts talking to you in the light language, she is attuning or activating you.

When you have been activated, you should be ready for your next session. It does not matter if you believe the process or not. Your healer is responsible for getting you prepared for the whole healing process.

Whatever you do, though, trust the process. It will not be easy if you are strongly linked to more scientific and logical reasons and methods. You can approach this new method gingerly if you must. Think about it. There must be something within you that urged you to explore this healing method.

Trust the process. This is a huge part of it. So, you must open yourself to receiving what is being sent to you. Nobody expects you to understand the meanings behind the sigils and the chants. All you need to do is to check if something is happening inside of you. Heavenly communication does not bother itself with logical and earthly meanings. A few more sessions later and you will start feeling a more specific change in you.

This is what happened to me. At first, I was confused and bewildered. I did not know what was going on. However, as time went by, a strong pull made me feel so much better. The depression slowly lifted up, but at least it did. I did not depend on medication, and I was glad that I chose that particular path.

How do you know there are various types of rituals offered?

You can inquire at your healer's office if she is offering various types of healing. Then, you can focus on the particular need you have each day.

Because of the COVID pandemic, healers are also offering virtual healing. Transmissions can happen through sound. The connection is through vibration. So, you don't need to be there, as you must for a medical doctor's clinic.

Some healers advertise their services as group chats wherein all the clients are muted while listening to their healer. Then, the healer will transmit the chants via the Internet through a preferred video call app.

It works. You also have to pay a small fraction of the usual cost of a light language healing session.

Can light language healing replace medical care?

Although the light language is the language of love, healing, and angels, it should not replace medical care. Take note that the individual body will show you just what you need. Some clients may find it easy to heal without any medication or medical intervention. However, that is not the case for everyone. Make sure your doctor is aware that you are also engaging in supplementary, alternative healing. This is especially helpful for those with some mental or emotional issues. While your healer wants you to connect to the illogical side of you, one nurtured by the Universe. However, she also does not want you to completely lose reason. This is not what light language is all about. In fact, it is about unifying what you know to achieve your greater self.

If your doctor sees that you are ready, you can gradually set medication aside. Similarly, you must also move progressively towards self-healing. The gradual change will provide you with the confidence that you need.

Remember that part of the success of light language healing is in your trust in the process. You need enough confidence to embark on your healing journey alone. However, there is also nothing wrong with having someone take you by the hand.

What are the types of healing you may experience when immersed in light language?

While the general process is the same across the healing rituals, some healers may define their services differently.

For example, you may be asked to choose among the following: angelic, sound, and energy healing. The intention here is the key to the differences.

Do you want to connect to an archangel to receive your healing? You may have to specifically mention this to your healer. The same goes for pure sound and energy healing. Whatever the case may be, these types of recovery are all about heavenly or supernatural voices helping you get better.

How can you heal yourself using light language?

As mentioned earlier, light language cannot completely replace medical care. However, it is a helpful tool in getting someone relaxed and ready for exploring the highest self.

Fortunately, light healing audio is being generously shared via the Internet. You can find some audio from YouTube and from healing websites. You can either stream or download these audios.

Then, you place yourself in a meditative state. Listen to the audio with your eyes closed. Even if you do not understand the words, focus on them. Usually, these audios use voices with a talent for singing. So, they are pleasant to listen to.

Chapter 4 – Ascending through Light Language

Not everyone is interested in light language for its healing capabilities. However, some mentally and physically healthy people want to pursue it to ascend

What is ascension, anyway?

Ascension, in our terms, is not the one that the Christian Bible describes.

In the Christian Bible, ascension happens when Jeshua rises to the heavens, body, and soul. While this may not happen to us in this particular manner, we will still ascend.

In light language, ascension means being able to lift ourselves up from our current position. With this description, you can say that healing is a type of ascension. However, there is more to ascension than just healing.

Ascension refers to being able to reach our highest self. In the business and leadership world, this may be described as self-actualization. Ascension is about being whole. It s about using divine communication to find the self that you are not meant to be.

Why is it difficult to ascend in this world?

A lot of us think of ascension as an earthly one. You get promoted at your job. You have reached a milestone in your marriage. Yes, there is nothing wrong with these achievements, but not all of them come with ascension. You got better at what you do, which is awesome, but you have not normally ascended. Ascension occurs when you use divine communication to reach the purpose of your soul.

The earthly achievements that we enjoy can be a result of manifestation. However, not all of them are rich with good intentions. Some may even be marred by false hopes and dreams. Sometimes, the things that we think we want are not really what is good for us.

How do you achieve ascension with the help of light language?

Different healers will approach ascension in a variety of ways. Some will look at it as a means to get to your core.

To build ascension, your healer may try to connect to your energy center. This has always been there but needs to be activated to achieve what it is capable of.

Yes, the thing is, you are capable of so much more than what you are gaining in your worldly life. Some healers may describe it as a phone number that is assigned to you. But are you even calling the number? Are you dialing up to connect to this core?

Some people indeed go about their lives with wasted potential. However, if you dig deeper into this term, you will realize that most of us are in this state. We are not doing anything to lift ourselves from the position that we are in. Instead, we have made ourselves content with our daily lives, dry and dreary.

This is why some people suddenly get the urge to look for themselves. But, of course, we often laugh at these people. Sometimes, we are even suspicious, especially if we are the ones who are left behind. Sadly, some of these new adventurers are merely finding a reason to go. But, of course, we cannot discount the possibility that some are being slowly pulled towards rediscovering their centers.

What should you do before ascending?

Before you even make up your mind to ascend, what it is that you want in life? Is there an aspect that you truly want to improve. Look at yourself.

If you are familiar with your seven chakras, you may know which among them is your strength and which is your weakness.

You may want to focus on a weakness first.

Now, each of these chakras come with a color and what it represents.

What colors can guide you through your ascension?

Red represents your physicality. Some people may have all that they need mentally and emotionally, but their bodies are weak. In addition, they are often ill, thus bringing down their endurance and stamina.

If this is your main issue, you may want to focus on the color red when attempting to ascend. This is your very grounding – your footing. You cannot climb further if you don't even have roots. That may seem contradictory to you.

However, think about it. How do you ascend into a greater plane if you are still trying to master your earthly one?

You may   want to get back to the saying, "the mind is willing but the flesh is weak." We often struggle to reach our peak when our own bodies fail us.

I remember when I was younger. I failed to achieve top marks because I was often sick. So, yes, the color red – of the lowest chakra, the root, also matters.

Then, there is orange. Orange represents creativity. Many people seek to ascend because they want to be in contact with more ideas. Writers, visual artists, and other creatives want this type of ascendance. Be careful when you are seeking this type of self-actualization. Ensure that the intention is selfless. The Universe may not want to help you ascend if your purpose is less than pure.

The same goes with Yellow. This color has something to do with knowledge and power. These are entities that are easily abused. Hopefully, you will express the need to attain them cleary. Show how you are trying to achieve power for the greater good. It sounds superheroish – but hey, the world needs more powerful dogooders out there.

Green, blue, indigo, and violet are closer to heavenly intentions. These colors represent the higher level chakras. If you want to ascend to a more spiritual plane, these are the colors that you must focus your energies on.

If you have moved on to a higher plane, focus on these colors. They will take you higher than before. This is true ascension.

What else can you focus on?

Though the above colors already represent the seven chakras, you may also directly target these chakras.

Chakra is an old Sanskrit word that means "wheel." It spins right inside of you. When they are balanced, you feel well. On the other hand, when they are not, you feel a sense of unease and loss.

A clogged chakra can bother you and may even prevent you from connecting to the Source. So, if you have been attempting to ascend using light language and everything has been failing, you must consider your chakras. Perhaps one or more are clogged. You will know which is blocked by the type of illness or unease that you feel. More often than not, you feel a literal imbalance when your root (found at the base of your tailbone) chakra is clogged.

Here are the locations of the other chakras:

Sacral chakra: below the belly button

Solar plexus: where your two sets of ribs connect with your chest

Heart: center of your chest, aligned with your heart

Throat: neck area

Third Eye: between your eyebrows

Crown: top of your head

This means that ascension can be focused on each of the chakras first. Even the chakras' arrangement indicates ascension, coming from the bottom (root) to the top (crown).

If you have any ailing chakras, you may need to go through healing first. This will allow energy to flow through your body more easily, going from the bottom to the top. Otherwise, you will still be plagued with issues that prevent you from understanding and speaking your own light language.

What does ascension entail?

When you activate your DNA through light language, you have already risen up. Ascension is about rising.

When a healer prepares you for enlightening, she does not have to do it again. This was mentioned before. You don't have to believe in it when it happened to you. Once you have been opened up for the experience, you are ready.

Sometimes, ascension is the result of something rough and traumatic. If you have gone through something traumatizing, your Kundalini energy may be activated. This also triggers the beginning of your ascension.

Now, here is where we have to be wary. Sometimes, a traumatic event can cause a powerful blockage. This prevents that person from being enlightened, much less being led towards ascension. Without support, many succumb to their situation and become hopeless.

The opposite is true for some people. Instead of being dragged down, they feel a sense of enlightenment. There is something within them that suddenly lights up as if to protect them. This automatic response is active in some people. They have strong psychic vibrations that make them open to the language of the Universe. Instead of experiencing blockages, their chakras may have allowed a sudden boost of energy to pass through the expected path.

Some of these experiences are difficult to define and understand. This is why they fit right into the world of light language. You feel a certain growing intensity within you that allows you to become more than you are supposed to be.

Instead of numbing yourself to the experiences, you suddenly feel everything more potently. You feel clarity instead of depression, clinging to the strong and positive awareness of everything that surrounds you.

When I went through my depressive state, I did not go through this, I have to admit. I chalk it down to the fact that I was born into a very scientific-oriented family. I was born into a family that scoffs at anything that cannot be explained. Because of this, I could not find any reprieve beyond what I could feel with my earthly senses. It was a suffocating time. I was later told that several of my chakras were clogged.

Knowing these for a fact made me envy those who have easily ascended after a round of adversity. There seems to be something so special about them. Their DNA seems hardwired to respond to negativity positively.

However, you must understand that ascension is progressive and sustained. Some people experience a sense of overwhelming peace and assurance, which is a sign of ascension. The problem is that it only lasts for a few minutes.

Then, they are back to the crushing reality of their current mental or physical trauma. While this may not be real ascension, it still makes a person feel a lot better. He will still remember and feel the consequences of his situation. However, the gravity may have been reduced. So, that quick dose of enlightenment somehow works.

True ascension will not only change you for a few minutes. Instead, it will change your way of life as you continue progressing. It can be a targeted ascension. You can specify what your problem is to your healer. On the other hand, if you are not sure of your situation, you can get a generalized appointment with your light language practitioner.

True ascension also entails a change in a person's whole lifestyle. So, a person may also change himself completely. He may stop having negative urges, such as vices.

What are the side effects of ascension?

But is ascension always positive? Does it have any side effects that make the patients feel a little worried about it?

Ascension and other types of experiences that deal with light language have minimal side effects. Some receivers may not even feel anything. This makes them uncertain about whether they have gotten anything from the session at all.

So, yes, you can come out of a light language session feeling no effects whatsoever. On the other hand, others may feel dizzy. Physical energy feels used up even though the receiver has been sitting down throughout the session. The receiver or client may also feel a tingling of his body, particularly the spot between his brows. This is the seat of the third eye chakra. The session has attuned him and has opened his third eye. He is now more open to transmissions.

Those who have already been attuned to the Universe before the session may have more overwhelming experiences. They may feel a deeper connection to the heavenly voices. As a result, you may expect tears and an overwhelming surge of emotion.

Chapter 5 – Speaking Light Language

You must learn how to speak the language. Yes, you can spend all your life going to a practitioner and receiving healing from her. There is no shame in that. People have various roles in life. These healers or practitioners have found it their life's purpose to attune receivers to light language. Once their clients are ready to receive the language, the practitioners can help them heal or ascend.

Sometimes, part of your ascension is being able to speak the light language. If you can feel this urge within yourself, you know that you are supposed to progress this way. You must ascend as a healer. As a healer, you can help others, or you can focus on helping yourself.

What can I give?

One of the biggest detractors to becoming a leader and healer is not trusting yourself enough.

Reluctant Speakers and Prophets

In the Christian Bible, even prophets had felt this uncertainty. Moses was afraid that he would not be able to speak well. He was not alone in this fear. Speaking is significant. You want to be able to convey wisdom with your words.

This is normal. We are still humans, clothed in flesh and blood. So, even when we attempt to speak in the tongues of angels, we are still afraid.

We ask ourselves:

- Am I good enough?
- Am I worthy?
- Will I be able to understand the language?
- Will I be strong enough to help other people?

Community and Sense of Sacrifice

When you take away the direct association with yourself, you can focus on the community.

Instead of asking, "what can I do to help?" question: "What does this community need?

With this, you give emphasis to the need. Yes, you are needed. People often want to be released from their blocked living. Some of them need someone to assist them.

Remember the first time you have tried light language? You do not know what was going on.

You were not sure what was being said. Therefore, you were not sure if the way you reacted was right. After a few more sessions, however, you were glad that you stayed on. You suddenly felt that freedom. It was almost like you had been released from the physicality of your body.

Medical Care and Support

It was the same for me. Someone I know was skeptical about it. This "friend" said, "I know that you had been going through light language therapy sessions. But are you sure they were the ones doing you any good? Aren't you also going through therapy with your psychiatrist?"

Her skepticism was actually welcome. It grounded me and made me analyze every step of my journey.

Light language has never claimed to replace medical attention. Instead, it seeks to supplement it. It connects you with something beyond this world. This belief system alone helps you rise above your situation.

When I was first diagnosed with depression, I immediately sought psychiatric health. Sadly, there had been a suicide in my distant family. I did not want to end up like that since I had people depending on me.

The good news was that the psychiatrist said that it was great that I took the initiative. Nobody else had to do an intervention with me. I trudged on – for myself and my loved ones.

The bad news was that I struggled with the medication. I was constantly anxious as a result. Instead of feeling down and sad all the time, I felt like I was living a fear-riddled nightmare. There was no sense of balance.

I also found out that because of my family history of heart disease, it was contraindicated. So, I stopped taking my medication. I was left with the option of non-medicated therapy. I had no issues with my therapist. However, I soon realized that it was getting expensive to be there regularly. Then, a friend suggested light language. She said that she was able to get rid of some negative energies from her life.

It was then that I suspected my sacral chakra was blocked. Hey, it took me a few meetings with my friend to discover just how chakras work.

It was the seat of creativity. Being in that field did not help. I was a bundle of explosive energy, always worried and eager to find something innovative. Whenever I was not creating something, I felt at a loss.

Speaking the language

I do not want to regal you with stories about how I immediately learned how to use light language. I did not.

However, I was lucky enough to be connected to a practitioner who knew her craft well. She was patient. Her calm voice eased me up. I did not know if it was a personal bias on my part that made me warm up to her quickly or if she really was just using light language to calm me down.

After three sessions, I was asked to speak the light language. I was terrified. How would I know what to say? How should I prepare? When I learned French in high school, I usually prepared like crazy before every class. I did not want to be called when I was not yet ready.

Trying it for the first time

First, a practitioner tuned me into the Universe. This is something that will happen only once. It is like taking a guitar and preparing it for use. Once you have been tuned, you are good to go on the next few steps.

*Once you have been tuned,
you are good to go on the
next few steps.*

Second, I attended some sessions. The
practitioner was aware of my depression. She
cautioned that I should still see my therapist,
even on a less regular basis.

She asked me to write my request on a piece of
basil leaf.

During my first session, I was just there –
overwhelmed and weirded out about how my
practitioner just broke into song and swaying.

By the second session, I started to tear up.
Something was going on. I still had no idea
what was being said, but I slowly felt the
rhythm in my chest. Something within my core
seemed to be responding, and I was no longer
afraid.

Third, I started vocalizing. I was responding by
sounding out with my throat. There were no
specific words, but I was mimicking my
practitioner's sound.

Fourth, I became proactive. My intentions had become clearer. I knew what I wanted as I started rising from the fog of depression. My goals were taking shape, and I was more confident with asking the Universe for them. I was not religious, but I could feel that my intentions were being passed on to a supreme being.

Fifth, I set my intentions free. I was no longer afraid of calling out to angels and deities. They were out there, flying out to the heavens. There was freedom in trusting something that you could not see but was feeling in your deepest core.

Sixth, I started receiving the transmissions with an open heart. I felt the difference, then. There was this belief that I was doing something strong and real. I remembered sobbing after that particular session. I was never an emotional person. Therefore, I knew that something broke down in me. No, it was nothing broken. Instead, it was something unclogged. I was free.

Seventh, I started listening to sessions on my own. Because I was no longer self-conscious, I was using all that I could. I sang, swayed, and even drew automatically. I wrote my intentions on sheets of paper that contained light language icons. I then realized that my connection to a Supreme Being was not limited by a practitioner. It depended on how open I was.

Eighth, I passed on the knowledge. Not being a healer by profession, I only did it with a friend who trusted me with his life. I made sure that he went through the necessary checks. Would the session affect his physical, mental, and emotional health negatively? Then, I would not dare put him through a light language session.

The last stage of my learning the language is writing this book. There is power in words if you know where to look. Hopefully, some part of this makes you curious enough to listen to a live or recorded transmission. Take this step. It might be the difference between living a life of despair and living as your highest self.

Conclusion

Thank you for reading this short introductory guide to the light language. Unlike a regular language book, you don't need to learn words and phrases. You just need to know how to let go of your physical inhibitions to welcome a world beyond your own.

May light language guide you towards healing and ascension. Then, when you are ready, hopefully, you will also pass on the knowledge to somebody else.

Made in the USA
Middletown, DE
17 January 2023